MEAT

MEAT

PERFECTLY PREPARED TO ENJOY EVERY DAY

This edition published in 2012

LOVE FOOD is an imprint of Parragon Books Ltd

Parragon
Queen Street House
4 Queen Street
Bath BA1 1HE, UK

ISBN: 978-1-4454-6754-2

Printed in China

Concept: Patrik Jaros & Günter Beer
Recipes and food styling: Patrik Jaros www.foodlook.com
Text: Günter Beer, Gerhard von Richthofen, Patrik Jaros, Jörg Zipprick
Photography: Günter Beer www.beerfoto.com
Photographer's assistants: Sigurd Buchberger, Aranxa Alvarez
Cook's assistants: Magnus Thelen, Johannes von Bemberg
Designed by Estudio Merino www.estudiomerino.com
Produced by Buenavista Studio s.l. www.buenavistastudio.com
The visual index is a registered design of Buenavista Studio s.l. (European Trademark Office number 000252796-001)
Project management: trans texas publishing, Cologne
Typesetting: Nazire Ergün, Cologne

Notes for the Reader
This book uses both metric and imperial measurements. Follow the same units of measurement throughout; do not mix metric and imperial. All spoon measurements are level: teaspoons are assumed to be 5 ml, and tablespoons are assumed to be 15 ml. Unless otherwise stated, milk is assumed to be full fat, eggs and individual vegetables are medium, and pepper is freshly ground black pepper.

The times given are an approximate guide only. Preparation times differ according to the techniques used by different people and the cooking times may also vary from those given. Optional ingredients, variations or serving suggestions have not been included in the calculations.

Recipes using raw or very lightly cooked eggs should be avoided by infants, the elderly, pregnant women, convalescents and anyone suffering from an illness. Pregnant and breastfeeding women are advised to avoid eating peanuts and peanut products. Sufferers from nut allergies should be aware that some of the ready-made ingredients used in the recipes in this book may contain nuts. Always check the packaging before use.

Picture acknowledgements
All photos by Günter Beer, Barcelona

Contents

Introduction

Meat – a staple food

Do we need meat? No, not really, as millions of perfectly healthy vegetarians prove. And yet most of us find it far easier to eat healthily if we include meat in our diets. Meat contains many valuable nutrients needed by the human body that are present only in limited or inferior form in plant products. To compensate for this, and to ensure their diet is not lacking in any valuable substances, vegetarians have to combine different vegetable foods.

Above all, meat is the principal source of the valuable protein we need for our immune systems, digestion and blood clotting, the transportation of nutrients, muscle and bone development and for our hair, nails and skin. 100 g/3½ oz meat provides an average of 20 g/¾ oz protein. Animal protein is processed better by the human body than plant protein because it is very similar in composition to human body protein.

But meat is also an important source of Vitamins B1, B2, B6 and B12, which regulate our metabolism, and Vitamin A, which is good for our eyes, as well as Vitamin D, which we need for our bones and teeth. Pork is an especially good source of Vitamin B1, whereas Vitamin B12 is present, above all, in beef.

Meat is also the best source of iron, which is more readily absorbed from animal sources than from vegetable. Meat also contains the trace element selenium and plenty of zinc. Like iron, zinc from animal products is absorbed more easily than from vegetable products.

To maintain a healthy eating plan, it's important that meat – like all foods – is of a good quality and that it's eaten in reasonable quantities. A maximum of three portions (150 g/5½ oz) of lean meat is the recommended consumption per person per week.

Apart from its health-related benefits, meat also has the advantage that it can be prepared in an abundance of ways and flavours. Virtually no other type of food is as versatile. Meat can be marinated, stuffed or coated, boiled, fried, grilled or oven-roasted, and served with a multitude of herbs and spices. It can be used in small quantities in sauces for pasta and noodle dishes. Combined with vegetable products, meat dishes guarantee us a balanced and, above all, varied diet.

Meat quality

Always look for meat that has been properly produced – this can be more expensive than meat and poultry that has been intensively reared, but it will be tastier and more nutritious. The following five criteria will help you check the quality of meat:

- Smell: fresh raw meat should have a neutral to slightly acidic smell.
- Moisture content: fresh, high-quality meat does not lose much water so should be almost dry, or moist only on the surface. Do not buy soft, oozing meat that is already lying in its own juice on the butcher's counter.
- Consistency: meat should be firm to the touch, not spongy. If you press your finger on it, it shouldn't leave a mark.
- Colour: fresh beef has a distinctive dark red colour, lamb is pale red to red. Pork should be pale pink and bright and shiny. Game, on the other hand, should be reddish to dark brown. Chicken is a light meat, and the skin and meat of corn-fed poultry are yellowish in colour. Duck is darker but should never be greyish-green.
- Fine marbling: the marbling pattern in meat is caused by streaks of fat in the muscle tissue. This fat content intensifies the meat's flavour during cooking. However, fatty meat is not good for your health in the long term.

Storing meat

Unpack meat wrapped in film or on polystyrene trays immediately after purchasing and cover and store in the coldest part of the refrigerator. Frozen meat or poultry should be thawed in a strainer and collecting bowl in the refrigerator to prevent bacterial growth. Thawed meat should be cooked within two days and, to be on the safe side, it should be cooked through.

Allow leftover cooked meat to cool and then store in the refrigerator. Never keep fresh meat in the refrigerator for longer than two days. If possible, mince and offal should be prepared on the day of purchase.

Meat in the kitchen

You should always wash your hands with hot water before and after handling meat. Thoroughly clean the sink and all equipment used to prepare or thaw meat after use. Use a separate chopping board that can be washed with hot water. Raw meat or melted water should not be in contact with other foods, especially if this food is not going to be heated.

When reheating meat dishes, do make sure the temperature of the meat reaches at least 80°C/176°F. Only temperatures above this destroy the majority of pathogenic germs. Meat, especially poultry, should always be well cooked to avoid the risk of salmonella poisoning.

Preparation

There are no set rules for cooking meat since each type of meat and joint requires a different type of preparation. Leaner pieces are often fried or grilled, while fattier, tougher pieces tend to be boiled or stewed. Finer pieces of lamb or beef should be cooked so that they are still pink inside. However, this is a matter of taste, and some people always prefer well done meat. Any type of meat mince, as well as pork, chicken and turkey, should always be well cooked. The following chapters contain detailed information about cooking and roasting times and recipes for all types of meat preparation so that you can find the methods that you like best.

How to use this book

Unless otherwise stated, the dishes in this book are intended to serve four.

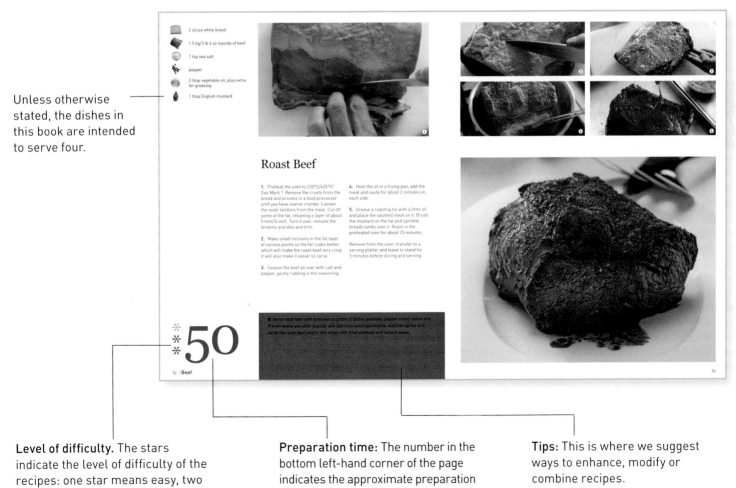

Level of difficulty. The stars indicate the level of difficulty of the recipes: one star means easy, two intermediate, three difficult.

Preparation time: The number in the bottom left-hand corner of the page indicates the approximate preparation time in minutes.

Tips: This is where we suggest ways to enhance, modify or combine recipes.

How to Joint Poultry

1. Remove the foot joints with a knife. Place the bird on a clean work surface, legs pointing towards you.

2. Pull the legs away from the body and cut to the bone with a knife.

3. Break the legs off at the joints and turn the bird over.

4. Remove the thumb-sized fillets and cut off the drumsticks.

5. Make an incision around the wing, about 3 cm/1¼ inches from the breast,

then scrape off the meat to the wing tip to expose the bone. Separate the wing with the back of the knife.

6. Carefully move the skin up so as not to damage it and loosen the wishbone with the tip of the knife.

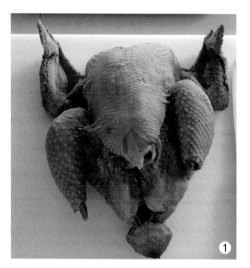

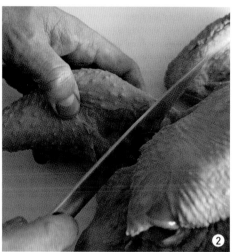

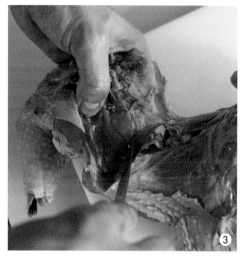

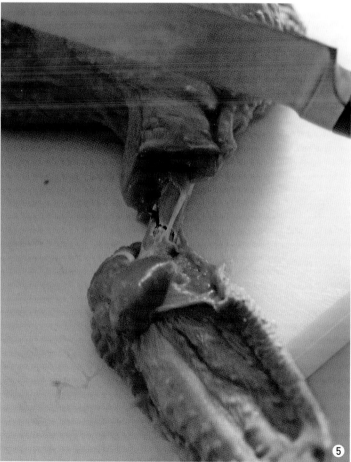

7. Carefully remove the wishbone. This will make it easier to cut out the fillet around the chest. Otherwise, you would have to cut around the wishbone, which takes a lot of practice.

8. Make an incision along the breastbone from where the wishbone was removed and cut from the abdominal cavity to the neck.

9. Use your hand to pull back the breast fillet and cut in such a way that the wing bone remains attached to the fillet.

10. Continue the process for the breast fillet, drumsticks and wings. Use the bones for soups or sauces.

■ You can prepare the liver and kidneys separately and serve them, for example, as a starter with lamb's lettuce.

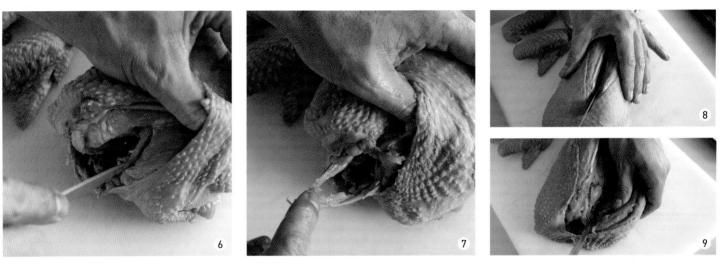

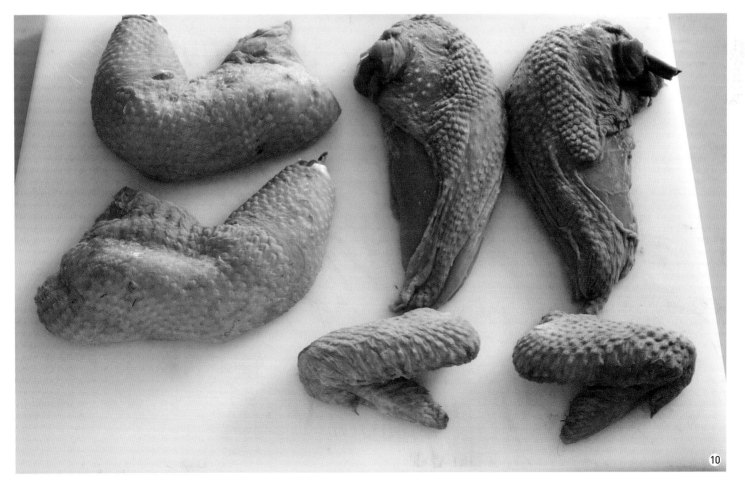

 4 skinless chicken breasts

salt and pepper

4 slices cooked ham

2 slices Gouda cheese or Gruyère cheese

100 g/3½ oz plain flour

2 eggs

200 g/7 oz fine breadcrumbs

6 tbsp vegetable oil

1 tbsp butter

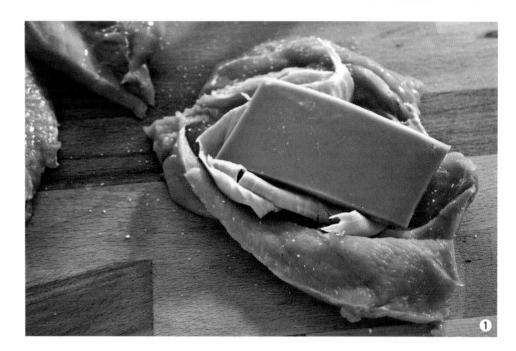

①

Chicken Cordon Bleu

1. Cut a pocket lengthways into each chicken breast. Season the breasts on both sides with salt and pepper and fill each pocket with a slice of ham and half a slice of cheese.

2. Fold the chicken breast over, enveloping the ham and cheese.

3. Seal any open spots and press the meat down a little.

4. Put the flour in a shallow dish and dip the breasts in the flour to coat, shaking off any excess. Beat the eggs in a bowl, then dip the floured chicken breasts in the beaten egg. Put the breadcrumbs in a shallow dish and dip the chicken breasts in them to coat.

5. Heat the oil and butter in a frying pan over a medium heat, add the chicken breasts and cook on each side for about 7 minutes.

Serve immediately.

■ To make the meat even more tender and tasty, marinate the cut chicken breasts for 2 hours in some natural yogurt mixed with a pinch of cayenne pepper.

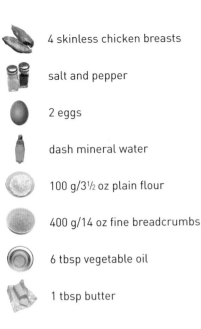

4 skinless chicken breasts

salt and pepper

2 eggs

dash mineral water

100 g/3½ oz plain flour

400 g/14 oz fine breadcrumbs

6 tbsp vegetable oil

1 tbsp butter

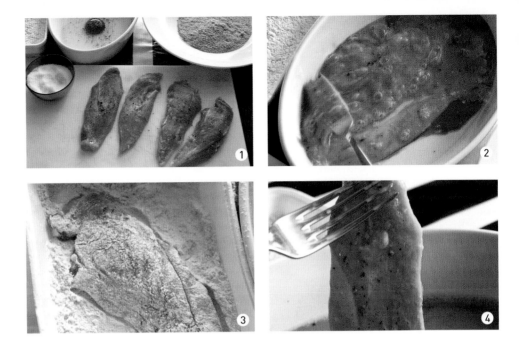

Traditional Chicken Schnitzels

1. Remove any fat or gristle from the chicken breasts. Season on both sides with salt and pepper.

2. Break the eggs into a shallow dish, season with pepper and beat in the mineral water using a fork.

3. Put the flour in a shallow dish, then place the chicken breasts in the dish and dust with the flour on both sides, shaking off any excess.

4. Dip the chicken breasts in the egg until they are completely covered.

5. Put the breadcrumbs into a shallow dish, then dip the chicken breasts in the breadcrumbs to coat.

6. Heat the oil and butter in a frying pan.

7. Place the schnitzels in the pan and sauté in the oil and butter mixture.

8. Shake the pan gently so that the fat covers the cutlets. This ensures that the meat gets cooked on the top.

9. After about 5 minutes, turn the schnitzels over and sauté for a further 5 minutes. Keep shaking the pan so the batter becomes really crisp.

10. Remove the schnitzels from the pan and drain on kitchen paper.

Arrange on serving plates and serve with a cucumber salad and lemon wedges for squeezing over.

20

■ You can bring a little zing to this recipe by adding 1 teaspoon of mustard powder to the flour.

 2 fresh rosemary sprigs, plus extra to garnish

2 fresh thyme sprigs

1 whole chicken

salt and pepper

1 egg

1 tbsp plain flour

80 g/2¾ oz white bread, sliced

3 tbsp olive oil

Baked Chicken with a Herb Crust

1. Preheat the oven to 200°C/400°F/ Gas Mark 6. Finely chop the rosemary and thyme. Joint the chicken and put the pieces on a chopping board. Cut the breast twice. Separate the legs at the joint and cut through the upper part along the bone. Season with salt and pepper.

2. Beat the egg in a mixing bowl. Add the flour, rosemary, thyme and some salt. Mix with a fork and work into a batter. Cut the crusts off the bread and process to fine crumbs in a food processor. Dip the chicken pieces in the egg mixture. Add the breadcrumbs and mix.

3. Place the chicken pieces on a baking tray and drizzle with the oil. You may have to cover the chicken with foil to prevent the herb crumbs burning. Cook in the preheated oven for about 20 minutes, or until the juices run clear when you pierce the thickest part of the chicken pieces with a skewer.

Arrange the chicken in a serving dish, garnish with rosemary sprigs and lemon wedges and serve.

■ To achieve a good crust consistency you must use really fresh breadcrumbs. Ready-made breadcrumbs are far too dry and will result in a hard crust.

1 garlic bulb

1 lemon

bunch fresh parsley

4 Cornish hens, each about 350 g/12 oz

salt and pepper

300 g/10½ oz small onions

60 g/2¼ oz butter

Cornish Hens Roasted with Lemon & Garlic

1. Preheat the oven to 180°C/350°F/ Gas Mark 4. Set the garlic, stem upright, on a work surface and press down with the palm of your hand to loosen the cloves. Remove the outer skin and crush the cloves in their skins. Rinse the lemon under hot water and cut into 5-mm/¼-inch slices. Pluck the parsley leaves off the stems. Wash the Cornish hens and dry them inside with kitchen paper.

2. Thoroughly season the hens, inside and out, with salt and pepper. Stuff with the pressed garlic cloves and the parsley, reserving some of the parsley to garnish.

3. Place the stuffed hens in a roasting tin. Cut off the stalk end of the onions but do not peel. Arrange the onions and lemon slices around the hens. Distribute the butter over the hens.

4. Roast for 25 minutes in the preheated oven. Add 100 ml/3½ fl oz water to the tin and scrape the base with a wooden spoon to loosen the sediment. Baste the hens with the jus and roast for a further 15 minutes. Remove from the oven.

Garnish the hens with the reserved parsley and serve with the onions and jus.

✳ ✳ ✳ 80

■ Be careful not to injure the skin when you pluck the remaining pinfeathers with fishbone pliers. The white meat would dry out at these spots. Cornish hens taste just as delicious cold. Serve with any type of potato dish.

 720 g/1 lb 9½ oz butter

6 eggs

1½ tsp dried marjoram

salt and pepper

½ tsp freshly grated nutmeg

 250 g/9 oz poultry livers

500 g/1 lb 2 oz white bread, thickly sliced

300 ml/10 fl oz double cream

1 turkey, about 6–7 kg/13–15 lb, with giblets

5 carrots

3 onions

3 celery sticks

250 ml/9 fl oz cider

750 ml/1¼ pints chicken stock or water

2 fresh thyme sprigs

Turkey with Bread Stuffing

1. To make the stuffing, beat the butter at room temperature in a large mixing bowl until creamy. Add 1 egg, the marjoram, nutmeg, and salt and pepper to taste and continue to beat until the egg is completely mixed in. Add the remaining eggs, one at a time.

2. Cut the liver into 3-cm/1¼-inch slices and combine with the butter mixture.

3. Cut the bread, including the crust, into 1-cm/½-inch cubes and put into a mixing bowl. Pour over the cream and leave to soak for about 10 minutes.

4. Carefully mix everything together with a wooden spoon so that the bread cubes retain as much of their shape as possible.

5. Preheat the oven to 150°C/300°F/ Gas Mark 2. Clean the turkey cavity well and remove the giblets. Season generously with salt and pepper inside and out. Stuff the turkey with the bread stuffing, but make sure that the filling does not come out at the neck.

6. Tie the turkey with string and place in a roasting tin. Cut the carrots, onions and celery into 5-cm/2-inch pieces.

+ 5 hours' slow cooking

✳
✳
✳

60

■ You can add cooked chestnuts, steamed apples, dried apricots or pieces of sautéed pumpkin to the stuffing. Served with sweet potatoes and cranberry sauce, it makes the perfect American Thanksgiving dinner.

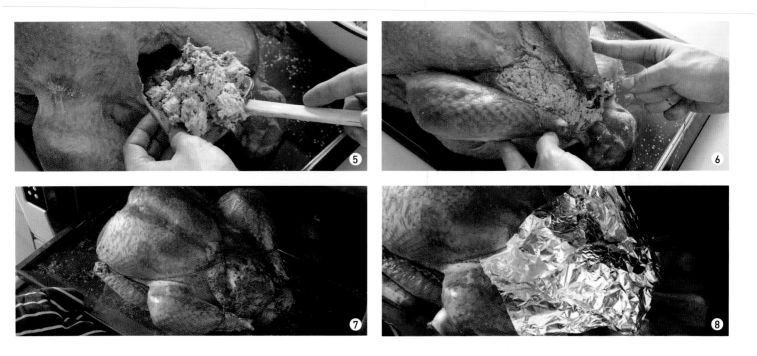

7. Pour the cider over the turkey and roast in the preheated oven for 4 hours, basting from time to time with the jus. You can thin the jus by adding some of the stock from time to time.

8. After 4 hours, lay the thyme and the vegetables around the turkey. Cover the stuffing with foil and pour 500 ml/ 18 fl oz of the stock into the tin. Roast for a further 1 hour, turning over the vegetables occasionally. Remove them from the jus and place them in a saucepan. Pour the jus through a strainer.

Place the turkey on a chopping board and serve with the jus and the vegetables.

4 duck breasts, 200 g/7 oz each

2 oranges

salt and pepper

1 tbsp vegetable oil

100 ml/3½ fl oz Cointreau

200 ml/7 fl oz orange juice

2 tbsp pickled green peppercorns

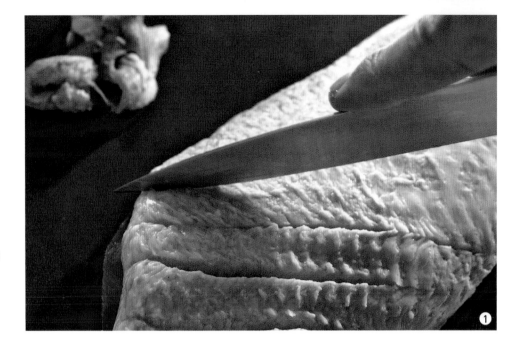

Roast Duck Breast with Orange-pepper Sauce

1. Place the duck breasts on a chopping board, skin side up. Cut off the protruding skin. Using a sharp knife, cut the skin in a criss-cross pattern.

2. Grate the orange peel using a fine grater. Use a knife to cut off all the pith from the orange, then slice the orange.

3. Season the duck breast on both sides with salt and pepper. Heat the oil in a frying pan and place the breasts in the pan skin side down.

4. Fry the breasts over a medium heat for about 10 minutes on each side, basting frequently with the duck fat. Continue to cook on the skin side until the skin is very crisp.

5. Arrange the duck breasts skin side up on a serving platter and leave to stand. Remove the fat from the pan, place the orange peel in the pan and add the Cointreau to the jus. Add the orange juice, peppercorns and orange slices.

Serve the duck breasts on warmed plates with the orange-pepper sauce.

■ Score the skin quite deeply to ensure that the fat escapes, otherwise the skin won't be very crisp.

*** 35

500 g/1 lb 2 oz pinto beans

80 g/2¾ oz carrots

80 g/2¾ oz celery

2 garlic cloves

80 g/2¾ oz onions

2 tbsp olive oil

4 fresh rosemary sprigs

3 bay leaves

1 tsp fennel seeds, chopped

1 tbsp tomato purée

200 ml/7 fl oz white wine

salt and pepper

2 litres/3½ pints chicken stock

2 duck breasts

Pinto Bean Ragout with Roast Duck Breast

1. Soak the beans for at least 2 hours. Cut the carrots and celery into 5-mm/¼-inch pieces. Press the garlic cloves into a bowl, then dice the onions. Heat the oil in a shallow saucepan, then add the onions, carrots and celery and gently sweat for 10 minutes.

2. Add the rosemary, bay leaves, fennel seeds and garlic and lightly sauté.

3. Push the vegetables to one side of the pan. Add the tomato purée to the centre of the pan so it loses its acidity. Add the wine, allowing the liquid to reduce.

4. Drain the beans, add to the pan and sauté for 2 minutes. Add salt and pepper to taste, then pour in the chicken stock and simmer gently for 50 minutes. Stir occasionally to prevent the beans sticking to the base of the pan. Stir carefully to avoid crushing them. Add a little water if necessary.

Meanwhile, cook the duck breasts (see page 20). Divide the beans between four serving plates, then slice the duck breasts, arrange on top of the beans and serve immediately.

+ 2 hours' soaking

* * * **80**

■ Fennel seeds are easier to chop if you drizzle them with a little oil beforehand to prevent them jumping. The pinto bean ragout also goes well with sausages or stuffed pigs' trotters.

Types of Pork Cut

The hallmarks of good pork are an almost ivory white, odourless, firm meat without moistness. It's not necessarily a bad sign if a piece of pork has two different colours. This can be due to the fact that a butcher made a cut at a crucial place, or it can indicate the stress levels of the pig before it was slaughtered.

Pork tastes best when it comes from free-range farms. This is particularly the case if the animals were fed on acorns and chestnuts.

The meat of intensively factory-farmed pigs ('turbo pigs') usually proves to be disappointing: their flesh is watery and they have enormous chops and hams. The flavour will be poor because the characteristic fat has been bred out.

There are hardly any reliable signs of quality. Nevertheless, when buying pork, you should make sure that it is dry and is not exuding any liquid. Meat that turns grey quickly also comes from intensively farmed pigs in the industrial sector.

For best results, the fat should be removed only after the pork has been roasted or stewed: it's an important flavour enhancer. If the pork has been wrapped in paper by your butcher, it will keep for about two days in your refrigerator at a temperature of 2°C/36°F.

In France, there is a well-known saying: *Tout est bon dans le cochon*; everything on a pig is good. Indeed, expert butchers know how to make full use of this animal. The blood is used in black pudding and the intestines are made into sausage casings. The breast meat can be smoked or cured.

The belly and the neck have far more fat than fillets; that, however, is not a disadvantage. As already said, fat is an important flavour enhancer. These cuts are inexpensive and lend themselves to long slow cooking, and are thus ideal for use in casseroles, stews and other substantial winter dishes.

Cooking Chart

Product	Weight	Method	Temperature	Time	Note
Roast pork with crackling (cut into the crackling with a razor blade)	1.8 kg/4 lb	Oven	180°C/350°F/ Gas Mark 4	100 minutes	
Rolled pork roast	1.5 kg/3 lb 5 oz	Oven	160°C/325°F/Gas Mark 3	110 minutes	
Smoked pork roast, uncooked	1.6 kg/3 lb 8 oz	Oven	150°C/300°F/Gas Mark 2	70 minutes	
Pork fillet medallions	60 g/2¼ oz	Frying pan	Medium heat	8 minutes	
Pork mince	2 kg/4 lb 8 oz	Oven	160°C/325°F/Gas Mark 3	80 minutes	
Suckling pig leg	2.1–2.5 kg/5–6 lb	Oven	160°C/325°F/Gas Mark 3	90 minutes	
Goulash	Large cubes	Saucepan with lid	Low heat	70 minutes' stewing	20 minutes' gentle sautéeing
Knuckle of pork	1.2 kg/2 lb 8 oz	Oven	180°C/350°F/Gas Mark 4	80 minutes	
Spare ribs	1 kg/2 lb 4 oz	Oven	160°C/325°F/Gas Mark 3	40 minutes	
Minced pork meatballs	500 g/1 lb 2 oz	Oven	180°C/350°F/Gas Mark 4	25 minutes	
Pork chops	250 g/9 oz	Frying pan	Medium heat	6 minutes	
Pork neck steaks	300 g/10½ oz	Frying pan	Medium heat	10 minutes	

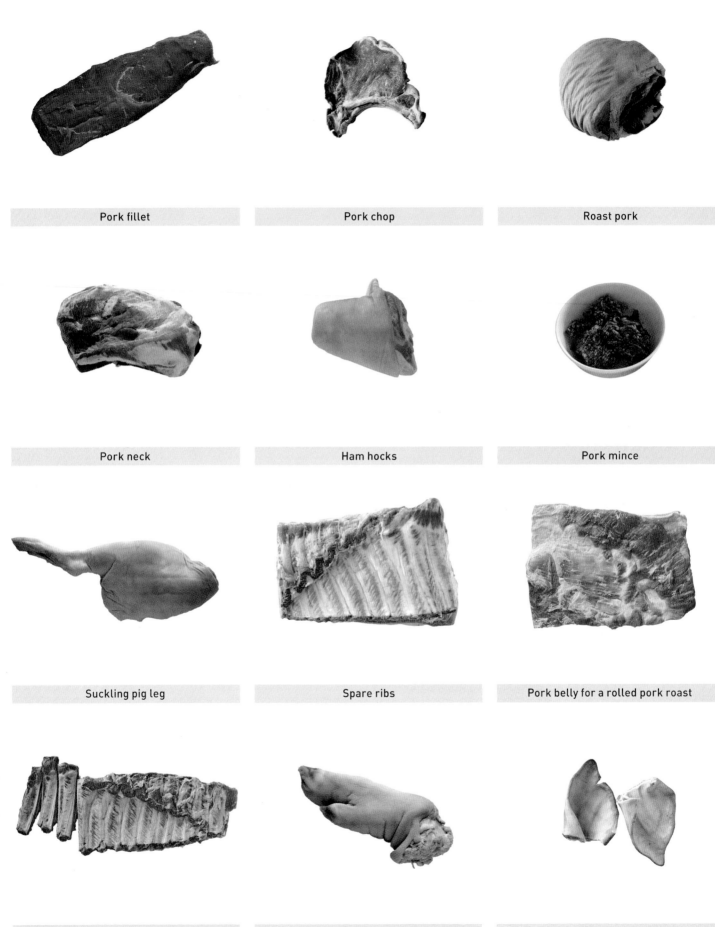

Pork fillet

Pork chop

Roast pork

Pork neck

Ham hocks

Pork mince

Suckling pig leg

Spare ribs

Pork belly for a rolled pork roast

Ribs

Pig's trotter

Pig's ears

- salt
- 1 onion, studded with cloves
- 2 carrots
- 100 g/3½ oz celeriac
- 1–2 suckling pig legs
- 1 pineapple
- 1 tbsp cloves
- 3 tbsp acacia honey
- pinch of cinnamon
- 2 tbsp vegetable oil

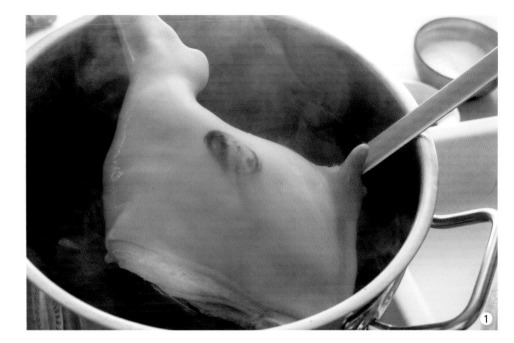

Suckling Pig Leg with Honey & Pineapple

1. Preheat the oven to 160°C/325°F/ Gas Mark 3. Bring a large saucepan of lightly salted water to the boil. Add the onion, carrots and celeriac. Add the pig legs and simmer for 5 minutes. Remove the pan from the heat. Remove the legs and leave them to cool on a chopping board. Reserve the pan juices.

2. Score the skin with a very sharp knife or a cutter every 1 cm/½ inch. Cut the skin off the pineapple, cut it into 1-cm/ ½-inch thick slices and set aside. Stick the cloves into the meat. This will give a wonderful flavour to the dish.

3. Put the meat into a ovenproof dish and drizzle with the honey. Roast in the preheated oven for 1½ hours, basting frequently with the pan juices. Lightly season the pineapple slices with salt, dust with cinnamon and rub with oil. Put them into a non-stick saucepan and sear them for 1 minute on each side.

Arrange the pineapple slices on plates with the pig legs on top and serve.

***180

■ For best results, use small suckling pig legs, each weighing 800 g/1 lb 12 oz. Two legs are needed for four people. Serve them with mashed potato, roasted beetroots, grilled sweet potato slices or glazed carrots. The sweet potato slices can also be added to the suckling pig legs half an hour before the end of cooking to absorb the pan juices to develop even more flavour.

- 2 ripe pears
- 1 tbsp butter
- 1 tbsp sugar
- pepper
- 2 fresh thyme sprigs, plus extra to garnish
- 4 pork neck steaks, about 125 g/4½ oz each
- salt
- 1 tbsp vegetable oil
- 125 g/4½ oz Gorgonzola cheese

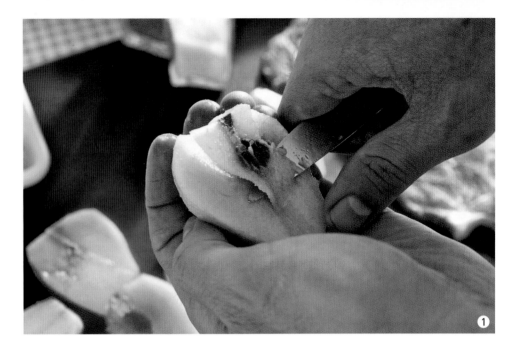

①

Pork Steaks Baked with Pears & Gorgonzola Cheese

1. Peel, halve and core the pears. Cut lengthways into segments.

2. Melt the butter with the sugar in a frying pan. Add the pear segments, season to taste with pepper and add the thyme, then toss until the mixture is slightly caramelized.

3. Season the pork with salt and pepper. Heat the oil in a non-stick frying pan, then add the steaks and sear on both sides. Transfer them to a baking dish.

4. Preheat the grill to high. Lay the pear segments on top of the steaks.

5. Put the cheese on top of the pear segments, place under the preheated grill and cook for 2–3 minutes.

Arrange the steaks on plates and pour over the pan scrapings. Garnish with thyme sprigs and serve immediately.

■ You can use dried fruit such as plums, apples or apricots cooked in red wine instead of pears.

500 g/1 lb 2 oz pork mince

2 tbsp oyster sauce

400 ml//14 fl oz canned coconut milk

1 tsp red curry paste

300 g/10½ oz canned sweetcorn, drained

2 tbsp flaked almonds

Pork Meatballs Cooked in a Coconut-curry Sauce

1. Preheat the oven to 180°C/350°F/ Gas Mark 4. Mix the pork with the oyster sauce and shape into small balls. Put them into a shallow ovenproof dish. Pour the coconut milk into a tall container.

2. Add the curry paste to the coconut milk and stir.

3. Using a hand-held blender, blend the mixture briefly, until the curry paste is thoroughly mixed in.

4. Pour the sauce over the meatballs. Sprinkle over the sweetcorn, followed by the flaked almonds. Cook in the preheated oven for about 25 minutes, covered with foil to prevent the flaked almonds burning.

Transfer the meatballs to bowls and serve immediately.

■ Milder yellow curry paste can be used instead of the red curry paste. A few petit pois can be added to the sauce as well.

2.5-cm/1-inch piece fresh ginger

½ tsp red curry paste

4 tbsp oyster sauce

3 tbsp vegetable oil

800 g/1 lb 12 oz pork belly

1 lime, cut into quarters

Grilled Pork Belly with an Asian Marinade

1. Peel the ginger and finely grate into a bowl.

2. Add the curry paste.

3. Pour in the oyster sauce.

4. Add the oil and stir well.

5. Slice the pork and put it into a suitable container. Pour the marinade over and mix well. Marinate the meat for at least 1 hour, so that the spices can infuse the meat properly. Heat a griddle pan over a high heat, add the pork slices and cook on each side for about 5 minutes.

Sprinkle the meat with the juice from the quartered lime and serve immediately.

* * * 80

■ You can also marinate pork chops or pork neck in this mixture and then cook in a griddle pan or under the grill.

1 ripe mango

2 oranges

1 white onion

60 g/2¼ oz butter

1 tbsp honey

6 green peppercorn clusters

salt

600 g/1 lb 5 oz pork fillet

2 tbsp vegetable oil

pepper

fresh Thai basil leaves, to garnish

Pork Fillet on a Bed of Mango Sauce with Basil & Green Peppercorns

1. Peel the mango, remove the fruit from the stone with a knife, and chop it into 5-mm/¼-inch cubes. Using a vegetable peeler, pare a strip of zest from 1 orange and finely chop. Squeeze the oranges and set aside the juice. Finely dice the onion. Melt 40 g/1½ oz of the butter in a long-handled saucepan. Add the diced onion and gently sauté until it is translucent, then add the mango cubes.

2. Add the orange zest and honey and gently sauté for a further 5 minutes.

3. Strip the green peppercorns from 2 of the clusters, reserving the remaining clusters to garnish. Add the peppercorns and the orange juice to the sauce, season with salt and simmer for about

10 minutes. Meanwhile, cut the pork fillet into 8 medallions.

4. Add the oil and the remaining butter to a non-stick frying pan and heat until foaming. Season the pork medallions on both sides with salt and pepper and add them to the pan. Fry on each side for about 5 minutes, basting with the pan juices from time to time.

Put portions of mango sauce on four serving plates and lay 2 medallions on top of each portion. Garnish each serving with a green pepper cluster and some Thai basil leaves.

* * * 50

■ You can replace half of the mango with pineapple when you are preparing the mango sauce, which will taste even fruitier. You can also use curry powder, ginger or chillies to season it more intensely.

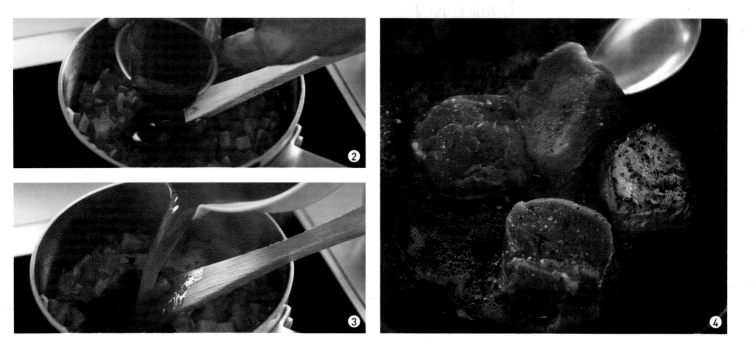

 1 small can or jar Mexican salsa

pepper

2 tbsp fresh rosemary

8 pork chops, 125 g/4½ oz each

2 tbsp olive oil

salt

Grilled Pork Chops with a Mexican Marinade

1. Put the salsa in a bowl.

2. Add some pepper and the rosemary.

3. Put the pork chops on a platter and pour the marinade over the meat.

4. Turn the chops and brush the other side with the marinade. Drizzle a little oil over the chops.

5. Cover the chops with clingfilm and leave to marinate in the refrigerator for at least 1 hour and up to 4 hours. Heat a griddle pan over a high heat, add the chops and chargrill on each side for about 3 minutes. Season to taste with salt.

Serve the chops immediately with chargrilled green peppers.

80

■ Buy a whole saddle of pork and cut it into 3-cm/1¼-inch cubes. Thread the cubes of pork onto skewers, alternating them with pieces of green pepper and sliced onion, and season them with the marinade. Grill slowly or chargrill on a griddle pan.

Types of Lamb & Game

Lamb: Good lamb is pale pink or almost white with a snowy white, solid layer of fat. This fat layer should be firm to the touch. If you are allowed to touch the meat, warm your hands first before sliding them over the fat layer. If the lamb is too old, your fingers will subsequently have the distinctive, pungent smell of mutton. A dull red, almost purple, or downright black colour is a bad sign. This kind of meat also comes from older animals and tastes like mutton. You should also be careful with regard to large chops or fillets. A normal lamb weighs 14–15 kg/30–33 lb. Anything heavier than 18 kg/40 lb is classified as mutton. Female animals are tastier than male. Lamb can be stored in the chill compartment of the refrigerator at 0–2°C/ 32–36°F for two days.

In order to enjoy really good game, you need to know a hunter. However, many consumers don't want lead shot or any authentic taste of the wild in their joint, so 'wild animals' are farm-raised nowadays.

Hare: Female hares taste better than their male counterparts. The males are tougher and more solid. The lighter the colour of the meat, the younger the animal. A red to a reddish-black colour is a sign of an old, tough hare. Young hare is more tender and is suitable for roasting. Older animals are better suited to marinating and slow cooking methods such as stews and casseroles.

Venison: Red deer, fallow deer and other deer that end up on our tables, are mostly farm-raised today. Males have dark, almost brown meat, whereas the meat of females is somewhat paler. The colour of fallow deer meat is similar to that of mutton. The smaller the animal, the lighter and more delicate its meat. As with lamb, female animals taste better than their male counterparts.

Cooking Chart

Product	Weight	Method	Temperature	Time	Notes
Leg of lamb	1.5–1.8 kg/3 lb 5 oz–4 lb	Oven	180°C/350°F/Gas Mark 4	100 minutes	
Lamb's liver	300 g/10½ oz	Frying pan	Medium heat	2 minutes	Cut into 1-cm/½-inch slices
Saddle/rack of lamb	400 g/14 oz	Oven	160°C/325°F/Gas Mark 3	20 minutes	
Lamb chop	60 g/2¼ oz	Griddle pan	Medium heat	5 minutes	Rub the chop with oil in advance, so that it doesn't stick to the griddle pan
Fillet of lamb	40 g/1½ oz	Frying pan	Medium heat	4 minutes	
Shoulder of lamb	1.3–1.5 kg/3 lb–3 lb 5 oz	Oven	200°C/400°F/Gas Mark 6	45 minutes	
Saddle of venison	Whole, 2 kg/4 lb 8 oz	Oven	180°C/350°F/ Gas Mark 4	35 minutes	Sear on all sides, in advance
Roast venison (female)	1.2–1.5 kg/2 lb 8 oz–3 lb 5 oz	Oven	160°C/325°F/ Gas Mark 3	45 minutes	
Knuckle of lamb	250–300 g/9–10½ oz	Oven	160°C/325°F/Gas Mark 3	90 minutes	
Roast venison (male)	2 kg/4 lb 8 oz	Oven	160°C/325°F/Gas Mark 3	70 minutes	
Venison medallion	60 g/2¼ oz	Frying pan	Medium heat	10 minutes	
Haunch of venison	1 kg/2 lb 4 oz	Oven	180°C/350°F/Gas Mark 4	25 minutes	
Rabbit	1.3 kg/3 lb	Oven	160°C/325°F/Gas Mark 3	40 minutes	
Saddle of hare	450 g/1 lb	Oven	180°C/350°F/Gas Mark 4	20 minutes	
Leg of hare	400 g/14 oz	Saucepan with lid	Medium heat	70 minutes	
Leg of rabbit	250 g/9 oz	Frying pan with lid	Medium heat	30 minutes	Stew

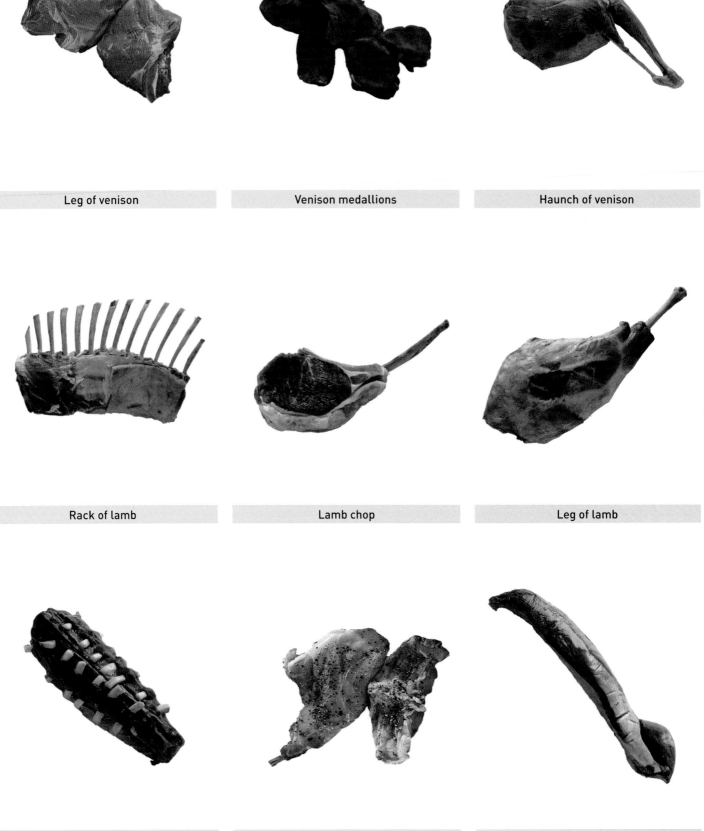

Leg of venison

Venison medallions

Haunch of venison

Rack of lamb

Lamb chop

Leg of lamb

Saddle of hare

Rabbit

Loin of venison

8 tbsp olive oil

2 tbsp fresh thyme

1 tbsp fresh rosemary

1 tsp fennel seeds

salt and pepper

1 leg of lamb, about 1.8 kg/4 lb, plus some lamb bones

1 garlic bulb

Roast Leg of Lamb with Herbs & Garlic

1. Preheat the oven to 200°C/400°F/ Gas Mark 6. To make the marinade, pour the oil into a bowl and add the thyme.

2. Roughly chop the rosemary and add to the bowl with the fennel seeds. Mix well and season to taste with salt and pepper.

3. Put the lamb into a roasting tin with the bones and rub the meat all over with the herbed oil. Separate the garlic cloves from the bulb, place them in a bowl and press down on them lightly with the heel of your hand. Put the garlic cloves on top of the leg of lamb.

4. Put the lamb in the preheated oven and roast for 30 minutes. Turn the roast frequently and baste it with its juices. Reduce the oven temperature to 180°C/350°F/Gas Mark 4 and roast for a further hour. While the lamb is roasting, add some water to the pan from time to time and use a wooden spoon to scrape the sediment from the base of the tin to make a sauce.

Arrange the leg of lamb on a platter. Remove the bones from the sauce. Pour the sauce over the lamb, and serve.

✳✳✳ **100**

■ Finely chop parsley, tarragon, marjoram, and lemon and orange zest and mix them with butter. Add to a frying pan, heat until foaming and pour the foam over the lamb.

- 2 saddles of lamb, 1–1.2 kg/ 2 lb 4 oz–2 lb 8 oz each
- salt and pepper
- 3 tbsp olive oil
- 6 garlic cloves
- 2 fresh rosemary sprigs
- 30 g/1 oz butter

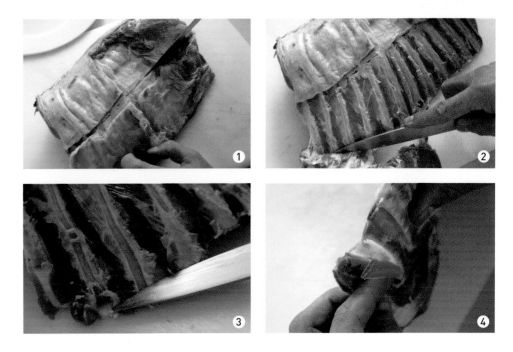

Pink Roast Rack of Lamb with Rosemary

1. Put the saddles of lamb on a chopping board and cut into the skin under the loin fillet at a depth of 1 cm/½ inch.

2. Trim the skin and the meat from the ribs.

3. Shave the skin off the bone with the knife, so that it is easier to remove.

4. Carefully loosen the skin from the bone with your fingers, until the bone is exposed and clean.

5. Turn it over and cut this part of the skin off.

6. Cut along the backbone and remove the white sinew carefully. Then continue cutting on the back to the ribs.

7. Turn it over again and separate the rack of lamb from the backbone with sharp kitchen shears.

8. Remove the small bits of sinew and bones from the separated rack of lamb and season it with salt and pepper on both sides.

■ You can use ready-prepared racks of lamb instead of saddle of lamb but you will still need to clean the ribs. The rack of lamb can also be roasted with a pecan-lemon marinade. Roughly chop some pecan nuts, cut 2 pieces of lemon zest into fine strips and mix them with 1 fresh rosemary sprig, 2 tablespoons of olive oil and 1 teaspoon of wholegrain mustard. Roast the lamb with this mixture for the last 5 minutes of cooking. Potatoes au gratin and French beans are very good accompaniments for rack of lamb.

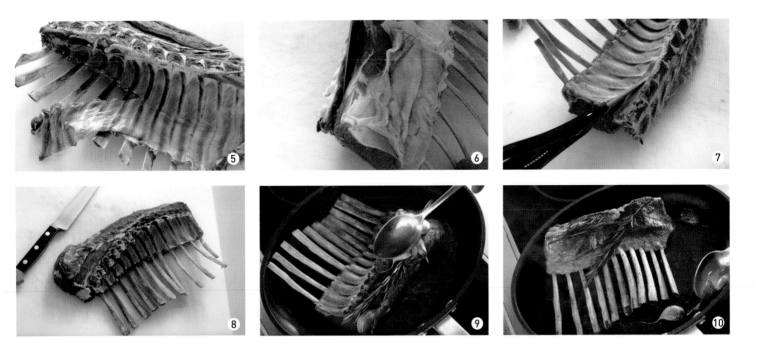

9. Preheat the oven to 180°C/350°F/ Gas Mark 4. Heat the oil in a wide, ovenproof frying pan and put the rack of lamb in it top side down. Place the unpeeled garlic cloves in a bowl and press down on them with the heel of your hand. Add the garlic and the rosemary to the rack. Baste the lamb with the pan juices and turn it over after 5 minutes, replacing the rosemary on top of the rack so that it doesn't burn in the pan.

10. Add the butter and roast in the preheated oven for about 10 minutes, basting frequently.

Remove from the oven, cover with foil and leave to rest for 3 minutes before serving.

1 leg of lamb, about 1.3 kg/3 lb

bunch fresh parsley

1 fresh tarragon sprig

5 shallots

150 g/5½ oz carrots

3 onions

1 head young cabbage

2 garlic cloves

300 g/10½ oz potatoes

2 tbsp vegetable oil

salt and pepper

½ tsp tomato purée

1 bay leaf

1.2 litres/2 pints beef stock

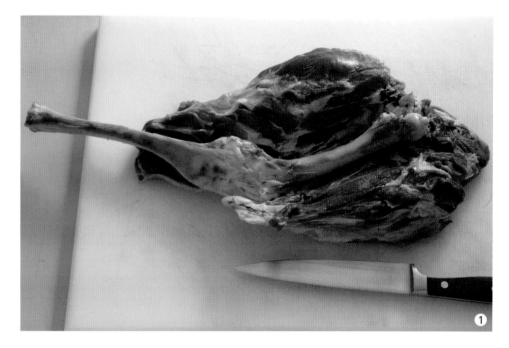

Irish Stew with Young Cabbage & Carrots

1. Cut into the leg of lamb along the bone and remove it carefully from the meat with the tip of your knife. Remove the fat and gristle from the skin. Cut the meat into 3-cm/1¼-inch pieces. Pluck the the leaves from the parsley and tarragon sprigs and set aside. They will be chopped shortly before they are added to the dish, in order to preserve their flavour and their essential oils.

2. Cut the shallots in half. Cut the carrots diagonally into 1-cm/½-inch thick slices. Halve the onions and cut them into strips. Remove the outer leaves from the cabbage, cut it in half, remove the stalk and cut it into 3-cm/1¼-inch cubes. Peel the garlic and finely chop. Peel the potatoes and cut into 3-cm/1¼-inch cubes.

3. Heat the oil in a saucepan, add the garlic and then the onion strips and cook until they are translucent. Season the meat with salt and pepper, add to the pan and gently sauté for 10 minutes. Push the meat to the side, add the tomato purée to the centre of the pan to brown it a little, then mix it with the meat. Add the bay leaf.

4. Pour the stock over the meat. You can use water as a substitute, but you will need to season the meat more if you do. Bring the stew to the boil, then simmer, covered, for 15 minutes.

120

■ Lamb shoulder can be used instead of leg of lamb, but it will have to be cooked for 15 minutes longer, as it is more marbled. The quantity of vegetables can be increased or other vegetables used according to your preference. French beans, celery and Savoy cabbage are every bit as delicious in this stew.

5. Add the carrots, shallots and potatoes and simmer, covered, for a further 10 minutes. Add the cabbage, mix all of the ingredients together and simmer for a further 20 minutes, then remove the bay leaf.

Finely chop the parsley and the tarragon, stir them into the pan, then serve the stew in soup bowls.

4 rabbit haunches

salt and pepper

3 tsp sweet paprika

2 small onions

30 g/1 oz butter

500 ml/18 fl oz chicken stock or vegetable stock

400 ml/14 fl oz cream

①

Stewed Rabbit in Paprika Cream Sauce

1. Season the rabbit haunches with salt and pepper and dust with paprika.

2. Finely dice the onions. Melt the butter in a wide saucepan over a low heat. Add the onions and gently sauté until they are translucent. Add the rabbit haunches and lightly brown.

3. Add the stock, bring to the boil, then cover, reduce the heat and cook for about 30 minutes.

4. Turn the rabbit occasionally. You may have to add some water if the liquid evaporates quickly. The base of the pan should always be covered with a 1-cm/ ½-inch layer of liquid.

5. Add the cream and simmer the rabbit in the sauce. You may need to add more salt and pepper to season the stew.

Serve with boiled potatoes or noodles.

■ A whole jointed rabbit can be prepared in the same manner. If you omit the paprika and add 250 g/9 oz of sliced mushrooms after you brown the rabbit, you will have a wonderful mushroom sauce.

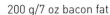

200 g/7 oz bacon fat

2 saddles of hare, about 400 g/14 oz

4 pears

salt and pepper

4 tbsp vegetable oil

10 juniper berries

5 bay leaves

2 fresh rosemary sprigs

40 g/1½ oz butter

1 tbsp soft light brown sugar

2 tbsp cranberry jelly

Larded Saddle of Hare with Cranberry Pears

1. Put the bacon fat in the freezer for half an hour or so. This makes it easier to handle. Remove the skin and the membrane from both saddles of hare. Cut the fat into strips 5 cm/2 inches long and 5 mm/¼ inch thick. Grip the strip of fat in the back end of a larding needle.

2. Carefully stick the point of the needle into the meat and guide it through until the bacon fat is evenly distributed in the saddle and is protruding slightly. Repeat every 2 cm/¾ inch. Larding makes the meat juicier.

3. Peel the pears, cut them in half, and remove the core with a melon baller. Leave the stem on the pear to make it more visually attractive.

4. Preheat the oven to 180°C/350°F/ Gas Mark 4. Season the meat with salt and pepper. Heat the oil in a frying pan, add both fillets and sear on one side, then turn them over. Transfer to a roasting tin. Crush the juniper berries, add them to the tin with the bay leaves, then lay the rosemary sprigs on top of the hare. Roast in the preheated oven for approximately 20 minutes, basting frequently with the pan juices.

✳ ✳ ✳ **120**

■ For best results, use small, red Williams pears. Serve the saddle of hare accompanied by small potato cakes, finger noodles or a mushroom cream sauce.

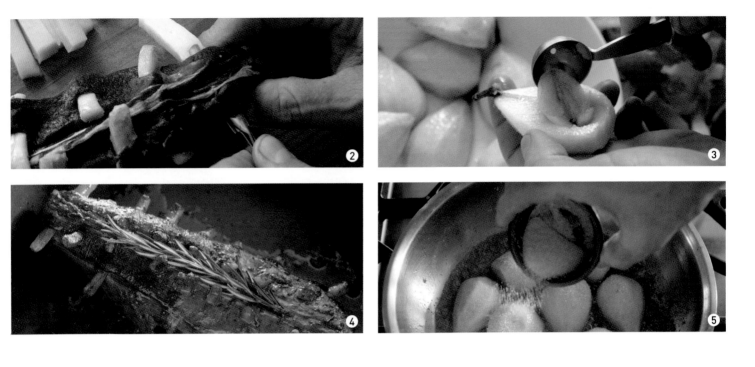

5. Meanwhile, melt the butter in a frying pan and sprinkle in half the sugar. Lay the pear halves in the pan cut side down. Sprinkle with the remaining sugar and slowly sauté until they are golden yellow in colour. Turn the pear halves over and fill them with the cranberry jelly. Carefully remove the hare fillets from the saddles with a knife and cut diagonally into 2-cm/¾-inch thick slices.

Pour the pan juices over the meat, transfer to a platter and serve with the pears.

Degrees of Cooking for Beef

Beef fillet steak

Rare/blue: The meat is sautéed for 1 minute on each side and is raw on the inside.

Medium rare/saignant/bloody: The meat is sautéed for 3 minutes on each side and has a pink centre with a bloody core.

Medium/medium/pink: This is by far the most common degree of cooking. The meat is sautéed for 5 minutes on each side and remains pink on the inside. However, the core is no longer bloody.

Medium well/à point/half-done: The meat is sautéed for 6 minutes on each side and is slightly pink on the inside. However, there are no bloody juices when cut.

Well done/bien cuit: The meat is sautéed for 8 minutes on each side and is well done on the inside. There are no juices when cut.

2 slices white bread

1.5 kg/3 lb 5 oz topside of beef

1 tsp sea salt

pepper

3 tbsp vegetable oil, plus extra for greasing

1 tbsp English mustard

Roast Beef

1. Preheat the oven to 220°C/425°F/ Gas Mark 7. Remove the crusts from the bread and process in a food processor until you have coarse crumbs. Loosen the outer tendons from the meat. Cut off some of the fat, retaining a layer of about 5 mm/¼ inch. Turn it over, remove the tendons and skin and trim.

2. Make small incisions in the fat layer at various points so the fat cooks better, which will make the roast beef very crisp. It will also make it easier to carve.

3. Season the beef all over with salt and pepper, gently rubbing in the seasoning.

4. Heat the oil in a frying pan, add the meat and sauté for about 2 minutes on each side.

5. Grease a roasting tin with a little oil and place the sautéed meat on it. Brush the mustard on the fat and sprinkle breadcrumbs over it. Roast in the preheated oven for about 25 minutes.

Remove from the oven, transfer to a serving platter and leave to stand for 5 minutes before slicing and serving.

■ Serve roast beef with potatoes au gratin or jacket potatoes; pepper cream sauce and French beans are other popular and delicious accompaniments. Another option is to serve the roast beef cold in thin slices with fried potatoes and tartare sauce.

- 5 juniper berries
- 5 white peppercorns
- 2 onions
- 175 g/6 oz carrots
- 175 g/6 oz leeks
- 175 g/6 oz celery
- 1 tbsp coarse sea salt
- 1 kg/2 lb 4 oz stewing beef
- 2 cloves
- 1 bay leaf
- fresh flat-leaf parsley, to garnish
- snipped fresh chives, to garnish

①

Beef Stew with Root Vegetables & Herbs

1. Using the flat side of a knife, lightly crush the juniper berries and peppercorns.

2. Halve the unpeeled onions and cut off the root ends. Halve the carrots. Cut the leeks and celery into 2 or 3 pieces, depending on their size.

3. Bring a large saucepan of lightly salted water to the boil, add the beef, bring back to the boil and simmer for about 1 hour.

4. Add the vegetables and spices and simmer for a further 1 hour.

5. Season to taste with salt and pepper and stir.

Cut the vegetables into bite-sized pieces and arrange them on a serving platter with the beef. Sprinkle over some parsley and chives and serve.

■ Serve with parsley potatoes, fried potatoes or creamed spinach. This dish tastes delicious with tartare sauce.

✳
✳ **120**
✳

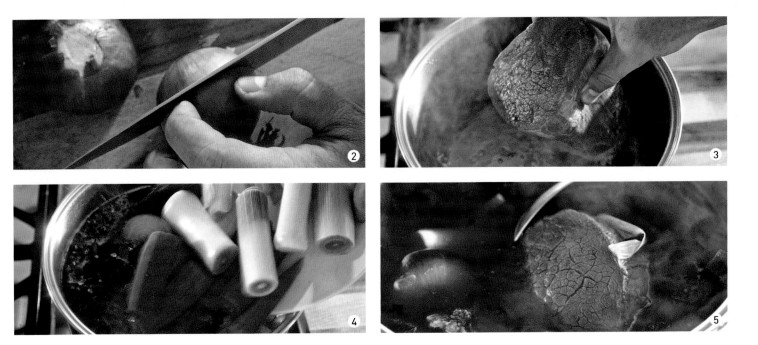

150 g/5½ oz carrots

1 head romanesco

150 g/5½ oz French beans

10 asparagus spears

2 tbsp coarse sea salt

100 g/3½ oz peas

½ bunch fresh chives

600 ml/1 pint beef stock

800 g/1 lb 12 oz fillet steak

salt and pepper

125 g/4½ oz cold butter

freshly grated nutmeg

Fillet Steak in Chive Bouillon with Spring Vegetables

1. Cut the carrots into 5-cm/2-inch pieces. Cut the romanesco into small florets. Top and tail the French beans. Peel the asparagus and cut into 5-cm/2-inch pieces. Bring a large saucepan of lightly salted water to the boil. Add the carrots and the French beans, then add the romanesco and asparagus and, finally, the peas. Cook until all the vegetables are tender but still firm to the bite.

2. Meanwhile, prepare a bowl of cold water and ice cubes to cool the cooked vegetables quickly and stop the cooking process. Remove the cooked vegetables from the pan with a slotted spoon and plunge in the iced water.

3. Pour the stock into a separate saucepan, bring to the boil and simmer for 5 minutes. Prepare the fillet steak and cut into 8 equal portions. Season with salt and pepper and place in the stock. Take the pan off the heat and leave to stand for 6 minutes. Remove the steak, transfer to a plate and cover with foil to keep warm.

■ Serve with fresh white bread, parsley potatoes or steamed rice.

* * * **60**

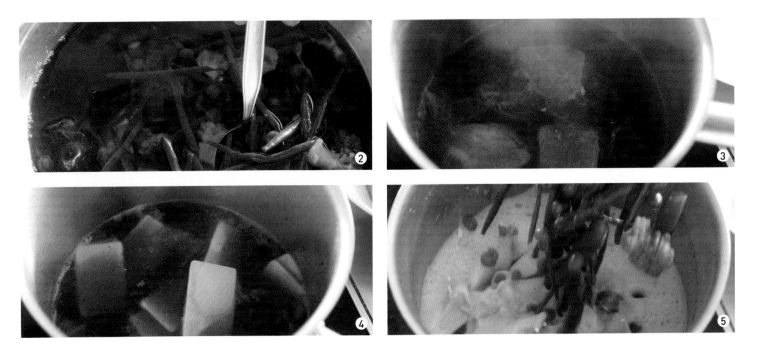

4. Slice the butter, add to the stock and bring to the boil. Use a whisk to thoroughly blend the butter into the mixture. Add the chives and season to taste with salt and pepper and nutmeg.

5. Drain the vegetables, then add them to the bouillon and reheat.

Arrange the vegetables in deep soup bowls, place the steak on top and serve.

- 750 g/1 lb 10 oz fresh beef mince
- 1 large onion, finely chopped
- 4 small day-old white bread rolls
- 500 ml/18 fl oz milk
- 2 eggs
- 2 tsp sweet paprika
- salt and pepper
- 1 tsp dried marjoram
- 1 tbsp English mustard
- 1 tsp cornflour, mixed with a little water

Meatloaf with Bread Sauce

1. Preheat the oven to 190°C/375°F/ Gas Mark 5. Place the beef in a bowl and add the onion.

2. Soak the bread rolls in a shallow dish containing the milk and an equal quantity of water for 20 minutes.

3. Squeeze the liquid from the bread rolls and combine them with the eggs, paprika, marjoram and mustard, and add this to the beef mixture. Mix well and season to taste with salt and pepper.

4. Place the mixture in a buttered baking dish and smooth with moistened hands.

5. Roast in the preheated oven for about 1 hour. Occasionally pour some water over the meatloaf. Remove the meatloaf from the dish and cut into thick slices. Add the cornflour and water mixture to the sauce and stir over a low heat until thickened.

Pour the sauce over the slices of meatloaf. Serve with parsley potatoes.

*** 110**

■ Add a dash of fresh double cream to your sauce. It tastes delicious and it stretches out the sauce, just in case you have more company for dinner than expected!

5 tbsp vegetable oil

3 cinnamon sticks

8 black cardamom pods

1 tbsp black mustard seeds

½ tsp star anise seeds

1 tbsp ground turmeric

500 g/1 lb 2 oz onions

3 garlic cloves

1 kg/2 lb 4 oz shoulder of beef

salt and pepper

1 tbsp palm sugar

400 g/14 oz canned peeled tomatoes

3 bay leaves

Indian Beef Curry with Black Cardamom & Cinnamon

1. Heat the oil in a frying pan. Add the cinnamon sticks, cardamom pods, mustard seeds, star anise seeds and turmeric. Lightly toast to intensify the flavour of the spices.

2. Cut the onions into 8 pieces each and peel and chop the garlic. Add the mixture to the pan and lightly sauté.

3. Cut the beef into 3-cm/1¼-inch cubes and season with salt and pepper and the palm sugar. Place the meat in the pan and sauté for 5 minutes.

4. Add the tomatoes and their can juices and the bay leaves. Cover the pan and gently simmer for about 50 minutes, adding some water from time to time

Serve with the toasted spices and some steamed basmati rice.

■ Create an Indian curry paste with the following ingredients: 3 red chilli peppers, 150 g/5 oz shallots, 5 garlic cloves, 10 g/¼ oz galangal, 10 g/¼ oz fresh ginger, 10 g/¼ oz fresh turmeric root (or use 1 teaspoon of ground turmeric), 2 tablespoons of coriander seeds, ½ teaspoon of star anise seeds, 5 cloves, ½ teaspoon of fennel seeds and 1 lemon grass stalk. First, grind the solid spices in a mortar. Add the other ingredients one by one until you have a paste. Use with fish, poultry or vegetables. Store in glass jars or freeze.

- 4 onions
- 2 tbsp sugar
- 1 bay leaf
- salt and pepper
- 100 ml/3½ fl oz fruit vinegar
- 800 g/1 lb 12 oz lean beef mince
- 2 tbsp oil
- 8 lettuce leaves
- 2 tomatoes
- 2 gherkins
- 4 soft sesame-seed hamburger buns
- 4 tsp mayonnaise
- 1 tbsp medium–hot mustard
- 4 tsp tomato ketchup

Traditional Hamburgers with Onion Relish

1. Halve and thinly slice the onions. Combine them with the sugar, bay leaf, vinegar, and salt and pepper to taste and place in a frying pan. Add 200 ml/7 fl oz of water and simmer for 25 minutes. The relish is cooked as soon as the liquid is completely reduced and the mixture has a jam-like consistency. Remove and discard the bay leaf.

2. Form 4 equal-sized beef patties. Heat the oil in a non-stick frying pan and place the hamburgers in it. Season to taste with salt and pepper and sauté for about 2 minutes.

3. Turn the patties over. Season again with salt and pepper and sauté for a further 2 minutes.

4. Slice the tomatoes and gherkins. Cut the buns in half and toast them. Put mayonnaise on the bottom half of each bun. Place a lettuce leaf on top and add 1 burger. Brush some mustard on the burger.

5. Add some tomato slices and top with the onion relish.

Place the gherkin slices on top, add some tomato ketchup, then top with the other halves of the buns and serve immediately.

■ Hamburgers are best served with fresh home-made chips. You can use other spicy sauces, cooked bacon rashers or fresh onion rings. If you like, add 1 slice of soft cheese to make a cheeseburger.

* * * 45

INDEX